Objects in Mirror May Be Closer Than They Appear

Poems

Gary D. Grossman

ARROYO SECO PRESS

Logo by Morgan G Robles

Arroyo Seco Press

www.arroyosecopress.org

Cover art: Gary D. Grossman

ISBN: 979-8-9918724-1-6

For my wife, children,
and writing colleagues,
to whom I owe everything.

Poems

I.

Bare Bones

They stand in the knife-like light
of the November moon. White and red oak,
mockernut hickory, and yellow poplar—
unclothed, their naked limbs reach
for both sky and each other—texts of
growth and admiration.

We are born naked and die naked—
bare skin opening and closing that
shimmering door—our alpha
and omega.

Clothing covers all, hiding truth.
But skin cannot lie, not now, not ever.

Permanence

At the end of Mom's last night I wondered how
thoughts traverse closed eyelids, and which memories

would last like white alabaster? I mean, there's
always another pizza after my wife

eats the last slice, even if I have to pick
up the phone to reorder. Do we still

say *pick up the phone* or is it just *where's
my cell* blurted to a now empty room,

the last person having left? And what about
the sole remaining Luxardo cherry

in the jar—original maraschino, though
they have no stems so you can't manage that bar

trick for last call, the one of tying a knot
in the stem using only your tongue. A flex,

documenting your value as potential
lover, if only for one last hour on one last night,

and will your ultimate amour be the last person
you'll entice into the empty atrium of your heart?

When you take them, will it be your last flat—this
current home, or will both lover and house slide

into the last chapter of your life's manuscript.

Was it Schrödinger who said everyone is both
first, and last, as well as someone in between?

Covering the Beds

Jack Frost begins his three day gig tonight when 12 AM temps fall to the age of college sophomores lacking AP credits. An eternal optimist, I winter garden, hoping to make Monet's brush strokes edible in my 320 square feet of French Biodynamic beds. Euphonious winter lettuces glow like ruby peonies or emerald-leaved camellias: Brune d'Hiver, Merlot and Red Sails. Kale cultivars embrace frost, and their sage-green to rosy bodies makes them as luscious as freshly licked nipples on an arching chest. With Mr. Frost imminent, I mosey out to the garage for my bed blankets; thin, muslin-like sheets of spun synthetic, that hug ground, and hold temperatures a few degrees above icicle air. Pulling these bed-clothes over my plants, I anchor each corner with a russet brick, discarded from my neighbor's last remodel, which leads me to thoughts about the barriers we grow ourselves to cloak true feelings: depression, abuse, languidness, and lust, and how these mantles vary in thickness from millimeters to inches—a smiling mouth with down-turned corners rather than tears. And yearning to peel back those mantles, like my garden covers, post-frost, I grasp that all we desire is a body three or four degrees warmer than our own, next to us in bed.

My Brother Ben's Office Souvenirs

Snow globes crouch on every flat plane:
window ledges, sills, shelving. Conga
lines of Lucite hemispheres: Hawaii,
Japan, Chile, Alaska, all proclaiming
I was here.

Their geometry recalls our upstairs
study—a shelter hijacked by January
ladybird beetles—marching ovals of spotted
marmalade—a filling, for the thin sandwich
of storm and standard windows.

The trees of the world are on fire, leaves
crumbling, but on a day with opal
skies, a shake of these globes helps reset
us—showers us with cleansing flakes
easing the reddened skin of daily life.

Cloacal Kiss

Mid-February and the red-tails
and red-shoulders dance across
the sky, shouting kiah, kiah
bird talk for *look at me, look at me.*
A pick-up bar in a cobalt
sky, with raptors circling and
chanting *hey baby, hey baby.*

Mating is a cloacal kiss
an uninspired and rapid
act of amour—white bread sex—
butts touching for just a few
seconds, male on the female's back
bending downward bussing his
cloaca with hers, and the next
generation is off to the races.

Cloaca, ancestral orifice,
a single opening for genital
and excretory pores. Birds, fish,
snakes and amphibians.

Which reminds me of the old adage
that humans must have been designed
by an engineer, because only an
engineer would have put the sewage
treatment plant adjacent to the
amusement park.

Artifact

Worst word in science, as in *not a real result*—experiment as bezoar
or reflux, hacked up by poor methodology. Sadly, the first
response of the hidebound lab, when discovery knocks, such as
gastroenterologists hurling poop on Dr. Barry Marshall for
concluding *Helicobactor* causes peptic ulcers. But the actual world
always prevails and my mouth now retastes chilies, and neat
single malt rather than scotch and milk at the local—
clarithromycin alone turns the key. Even in poetry, genius begins
as atoms no one else has cleaved.

Adolescence

Imagine this,
I'm fourteen, home from a weekend trip,
smiling at the lemony rays of an LA
December afternoon, then turn the key
in the worn brass plated doorknob.

Imagine this,
my nostrils are punched by fists
of shit and vomit, and I wonder how
some cat or coon entered the apartment
and died.

Imagine this,
Mom's lying in the mess, uncapped
amber pill bottles lined up like soldiers
in a firing squad on her nightstand.

Imagine this,
it's not the first time.

Guy in a Thin Blue Parka Doing Tai Chi in the Last Available Parking Spot in the Restaurant Lot.

I get it—Cape Cod, and you want the ocean
to lick your face, not like a dog, but as a new
baby gumming your cheek, because this
is the heart's least cluttered promise.

It is early April, wind offshore, temperature 39°F.

The beach nestles just over the lot retaining
wall—mottled with seaweed, water-scrubbed
pebbles, and white, white sand. If you squint,
it turns into a variegated 80s den carpet,
the ones patterned to hide dirt.

Tai chi is beyond me. I know only that it exhales
flexibility and tranquility, but this guy issues
a pointedly bovine grunt every time his arms rise
above his shoulders, hands clasped in some sort
of prayer pose. Oddly, it seems like *enraged tai chi*—
as if strong wants and moving limbs could somehow blend
karmically, flooding his corporeal chi with endorphins.

We've circled the parking lot three times
to no avail, and here on the Cape, parking,
as well as other things, are at a premium.
Hunger plays an out of sync kettle drum
in three different digestive tracts, as we edge
the Subaru into this last space, thinking surely
someone so mindful will grasp what is
happening—we couldn't be more wrong.

Waiting and watching, we discuss modes
of communication, all the while trying to avoid
being judge and jury while he jerkily
repeats several rounds of poses, every one
ending in prayer.

9

Finally, Rob lowers the window and quietly yells,
we'd like to park in this spot. The guy peers back
at us as if we were the last three passenger pigeons
in the Massachusetts of 1894, then moves to the right
and resumes prayer pose in front of the adjacent car.

It is warm in the restaurant, as we inhale
the chunky perfume of fresh chowder.

Rising at 5:47 AM

I'm standing, chill air drawing my silhouette, in the unlit sea-green
bathroom—the halting walk from bed to bathroom sink has
        unfurled my
wakefulness—and I slowly open the corner of my reflection on the
        medicine
cabinet door. Daily doses are located by position and size of their
        child-proof
containers. Their shapes and colors vary like microscope images of
        sand, chunks
of chemical rainbow, these morning pills now held tight in the
        hollow of my
palm: circles, rectangles, and triangles, milligrams to grams; as I
        juggle both
water cup and tap handle, hoping not to dislodge a single caplet.
        The cup fills, like
the shade lifting on the morning sky, and I bring my health-
        bearing hand up,
tossing those small physiological correctors into my mouth. I sip
        and swallow,
then return to now cool sheets—the new day yet unmade.

Pulling Carrots

It's March 18th and despite the ground
freeze last Saturday, our carrots crave
assessment—the scent of ripeness
hovering over the bed of orange, red
and purple heads poking up through
a roof of crushed pine bark.

The secrets of root vegetables arouse me.

Always a hidden story: a disputed
recitation.

Seeds sown last October, but winter's
wardrobe was unhemmed, cool, and bright
enough to sugar these vegetal fingers.

Now feathery leaves sew the spring breeze,
their scent a lurid promise. I pull one from
the largest bunch, parting a wave of soil—sand
grains dripping off the root. It is straight,
thick and half a foot long—a clandestine
happiness, like the first kiss of a new lover.

Moving through the bed, I hope for sticks
of vegetal candy, not crooked old roots—
fibrous and bitter as a sixty-year-old
bachelor.

Moving to the next patch, I wait for
the touch of the earth's second secret.

Frog Shrouded

Is that what she actually said,
frog shrouded? Poetic for sure
but what is the necessary
specificity—medium-sized
leopard frogs, or large bullfrogs,
maybe tiny gray tree frogs,
a blockade crawling upwards with
hexagonal mucous-celled toes,
like small wind-up toys?

My hearing, well at three score and ten,
things do go awry. I'm sure of what
she said, but her mic echoed, and her
voice at eighty-two, is soft. Later, I laughed,
of course, she said *fog shrouded.*

Magic

The toilet runs faster than I can, though Devin the plumber hung a new flapper valve yesterday and repatriated the handle lever to its proper home in our ceramic tide pool, but for the last twenty-two minutes, I've been fooling with a babbling brook instead of Walden pond. I get it. Required is some spell beyond the handy-dad castings of my ten fingers, and Devin: well tomorrow—and as I'm reseating the ceramic lid, the strands of sunlight peer down through our slatted bathroom blinds, only to hook down into my cerebellum, snagging a fifty-year-old memory of making gels for starch electrophoresis—the birth-moment of gene variant classification. A hand-scribed chemical recipe my biblical codex, I mix reagent grade corn starch with twice-distilled water, add heat, and tune my ears for just the right hiss as the syrup de-gasses— then pour the molds. More often than not, the end is whey not curd. Same formula, same technique, magic again, I suppose. Students, we barely had quarters to rub together and only owned a 60s era Peugeot 404 wagon, that gasped, then halted every two months. I would replace parts, reseal gaskets, purge and repurge vacuums, only to find—problem solved three times out of five, though no conjure crossed my lips.

Where is that spell to make every kiss, every repair, every word, spark the very first time?

Bruised Old Apples

Like the thirty-eight dollar rondels at
Le Fromage Vert, Mom had a double-cream
illness—a paste of depression, tightly
waxed with a rind of mania. But fifty-four

years later, what remains are blurry mental
videos of her form, a sheer aqua nightgown
lying in puke and diarrhea—as if shot from
the last car of my bullet train of memory.

My wife says I'm less bruised than most old apples.

But doubt still sails my briny brain weekly,
and I can't help but wonder if trauma
ever really heals, or just remains as hardened
layers of shellac on the interior walls of my skull.

My cell pings—a text from my youngest,
the neuroscientist.

Impulse Control

Strong impulse
control means

missing
the blood moon

of November,
the Coho

Salmon that
just jumped

the falls,
and the tickling

wind of March
across bare skin.

Symmetry

Remembering,
glee, and relief,
when the youngest child
slept through the night

little did I know the
emotions would resurrect
in my heart, at 63
when I managed the same.

One Degree of Separation

The apple doesn't fall far
from the tree, *right*? But a microburst
day might blow it to some exotic
orchard, say kiwi, or dragon fruit.
Which is how Sylvia Plath's

and Ted Hughes' son, Nick, chose
fish behavior rather than poetry. In
my own poetic vacancy — the age
between high school and early
career, Plath, post-mortem summited

every feminist peak, while Hughes
was deemed part beast, part poet-
laureate. I knew neither. Nick,
then colleague, rarely mentioned
family — Ted and Sylvia mere motes

in the milieu of fisheries
biology. Our shared research love
was lithesome and fickle — we explored
why stream fishes chose and held
specific positions in flowing water —

our papers adorned with terms
like: capture success, reactive
distance, energy maximization.
We dined on pulpo ala Gallego
and almejas while chatting about

our session at the stream fish meetings
in Luarca, Spain: afterwards penning
a joint review*. I was a decade
older, and his Dean emailed —
tenure evaluation? With pleasure

I replied, despite the caveat
letter will be public. Nick's papers
read like Shelley's sonnets, dog-eared
in my library, the letter flew off my printer,
circled once, and entered the gravitational

field of University of Alaska: Tenure quickly
granted. Next month a case of wine
sans sender knocked on my door.
Confirmation received from Nick's
smile, reaching almost to his ears.,

Repeated gaps in contact and
I thought *genetic depression*,
but Nick could still pull rebounds
off the boards—until he couldn't.
Like Antigone, Oedipus Rex,

or the Book of Job, we all run
the familial race, some longer,
some shorter, but always till the end,
because the apple really never
does fall far from the tree.

*P. A. Rincón, N. F. Hughes, and G. D. Grossman. "Landscape approaches to stream fish ecology, mechanistic aspects of habitat selection and behavioral ecology. Introduction and commentary." Ecology of Freshwater Fish 2000: 9:1-3.

Valentine's Day

The February air—a cobalt needle
suturing the carmine cuts of winter. My lips

angle upwards, as I watch the sky turn itself
inside out, revealing the gnarled hands

of some awakened god who's just discovering pity.
Flying in and out of small holes in the sky,

hawks cut tight donuts around each other, pairs of
red-shouldered and red-tailed, they twirl an indiscreet

dance, calling kiah-kiah-kiah—eyeless
for anything other than themselves. The birds

shape a rusty funnel of desire—at the peak
the male mounts the much larger female, and both

come as they hurtle ground wards—next generation
passing—him to her.

As all should be—two bodies entwined—
release, and a soft blue sky?

Will You Buy My Book?

Welcome to the reading tonight by John Buck,
who needs no introduction. John will you say
a few words to start us off?

I write mostly in blank verse, trying to
capture the luxury found in everyday
actions and experiences.

will you buy my book,

my writing is metered but not formal,
no sonnets, cinquains or villanelles.

will you buy my book,

favorite subjects are birds, flowers, kids,
relationships, and running, sometimes
I combine all four,

will you buy my book,

And I'd like to end my introduction by
thanking my host, Jane Smith, for this
invitation, and all of you for attending,

will you buy my book,
will you.
Will you please?

The Oracle Speaks

At the back of the thrift store, in the peripheral vision of my right eye, a clerk is dusting off a Magic Eight Ball. With every swish, two years erase from this mid-20th century prophet, then a sudden squall of mental wind sweeps me back to 1972 and LA, couched in Jules living room, her parents away at their Malibu beach house. Linda, her sister, stands and cools in front of the open refrigerator in matching black lace panties and bra. She asks *is there any pie left, I could eat a horse?* Her blood sugar at ebb tide, an aftereffect of the three bowls of Michoacán we've just finished smoking. Jules brings out her Magic Eight Ball, our Pythia of Delphi, with its score of answers varying from *reply hazy, without a doubt,* to simply, *NO.* It is our *go to* when befuddled and baked, and I am befuddled on whether to transfer to university at Berkeley, leaving Jules, the first owner of my heart, behind. I query, shake the Eight Ball, turn it over, only to read a definitive *NO.* Both left and right corners of Jules mouth slowly slide upwards. Facing the girls I say *The last time I used the Eight Ball, it told me not to go to college.* And *bang*, like a power line transformer exploding in Georgia's August heat, I rematerialize in the store, shake my head left and right to clear it from my decade's old abandonment of Jules and the oracle, and then recall the Wednesday in 1987 when I was granted tenure at the university down the street.

II.

The Mockingbird and the Worm

It's a matter of survival,

perching on this cypress mailbox
 post after the dousing, two
  inches at least, no crunchies, nor
  flyers, but a wondrous day for
   many-legs and slimy skins
    as I shake my wings dry
     again, shedding rain drops—
     when I spy a slimy-skin,
      and flush downwards, only to
       strike a void of rain-beaded
        grass
       then relaunch to the
     cypress perch, and my
eternal search for prey

slithering through the fescue,
   unsharpened by the steely rain—
      today I can go anywhere
   my home-earth wet-green,
and venturing out
   out to taste new ground—
      a sudden shadow, I shimmy
   to the right, avoiding
the strike-beak—gray-white
   wings buffeting the damp grass,
      as the puzzled bird cocks its
   head from side to side, then
lofts again to join the shadowed
   world above.

It's a matter of survival.

24

Nest Failure

Every March our resident Wrens
botch their nest-making, building on
the four by four inch cross-tie under

the side-porch roof. *Get it right* I tell
these feathered golf balls, who already
have fled—a blurred beam of burnt sienna.

Facilely smart, they grasp a haven,
lacking cats, coons, and even cowbirds,
but our family's comings and goings

scare, chaotic, disjunct—they shift avian
crania into fear gear. *This is so sad* I say,
foot-pushing their doting house of
woven moss, oak and beech leaves,
off the edge of the gray porch floor.

MRI

Modern medicine says hello, not with a smile or twinkling eyes,
but with a bang loud enough to wrench my head ninety degrees to
the left, as if Rowdy Roddy Piper had me in a headlock, while the
referee slaps the mat, the count now at eight. But no, my head is
hugged by two expensive plastic braces—penny-level expensive
compared to this bedroom-sized multi-million dollar machine, that
is making every kind of bang, clang, and soft-tissue image
possible. Then there's the high pitched shriek that I myself would
issue, if any utterance was permitted, however, my imperative is to
remain motionless as a bullfrog within reach of a hungry great
blue heron, and so I just repeat my mantra and loosely clutch the
blue squeezy that activates the escape protocol. Wedding ring and
Maori jade amulet removed and I'd better ask about the titanium
staples that have merged the sections of my lower colon for the last
35 years, because metal is metal, regardless of where it sleeps, and
this machine hugs tight to metal as if it were the only lover in the
Imaging Center. Loose, comfortable clothing they say, so it's tee
and running shorts—medicine is always cold in both affect and
effect, so it's a long-sleeved tee rather than a shorty. Surprisingly,
the tech says *after a while your back may grow hot* because my back is
what I'm here for, well, spine specifically. And I won't bore you
with terms like L4 subluxation and collapsing spinal canal, because
I can still walk, even while my nerves fire hot shots through
weakened legs to my toes, and it may be that pins and needle soles
will be my new story for decade eight, even though a scalpel waits
to write the opening paragraph.

Bloodroot in March

1.
Regardless of the year, it's the first
flower seen on my daily hikes, pushing

through every November's abandoned
duvet of tan and umber—a patchwork

of ash, oak, maple, and hickory. I pause,
eyelids unspooled, like a tired window

blind, and inhale the forest's green
anticipation.

2.
Willingly, this could be my last breath—
absorbing the effortless geometry

of these eight ivory petals, rising
from leaves mimicking round Japanese

fans from the 1840s.

3.
How is it that small perfections can
both break and reassemble us—as

if we were Adam or Eve on day one
of the completed world—mouths agape

at the very first ivory petals.

Sprouting Onions in the Kitchen

Who among us hasn't received the
overdue notice from the last two
yellow onions in the five pound bag;
now spouting green Vesuvial
eruptions from the kitchen hanging
basket and chanting *some days,*
enough is just too much.

Who among us hasn't worn regret's
papery skin at words unsaid, actions
unbegun? The *love yous* and hugs that now
float down-river, caught perhaps in remnants
of a green mesh plastic sack, like the one
now holding these two flaccid onions.

Who among us hasn't named regret—
brother, sister, or first cousin, though
tomorrow, and all days thereafter,
are a kitchen counter wiped clean:
a floor just swept.

Softness

My Mother passed down guilt and the work ethic,
heirlooms that serve through crisis and calm. When

my wife and I met, our pockets held nothing
but palms—*it's the thought that counts.*

To her I passed down tee shirts, well-worn, gentle
as nightingales' feathers—repurposed as nightgowns,

winter and summer. Then two girls knocked on her wombs
door—popped out, and four point seven years later

inherited my tees—shirts climbing the stairs of one
more generation—now floor length over five-year-old

twig legs. Are these cotton shirts safe harbor for my cells
and genes? Are they shield and armor against plague

and nightmare—though soft as tulle? I watch as the older
sucks the pliable neck-ring into her mouth in the universal

need to suckle. Can she taste my imprint—the decade - long
sagas of my life?

How does such softness hold the granite sheets of love?

The Count

Trapped in plane or party, when interest lags like duckweed
blown to the corner of Audubon's pond, I start a game. Call me
churlish, though not true because the play is hidden, like the way
sheep don't know they're being led to slaughter because there is no
blood smell. Of course, no murder happens here and my partner
has no ego sheared off, unless they sense the flippancy of final *so
nice speaking with you.* Narcissism is common and fluffy as cold
snow on a December night, Borderline Personality, same—both
can play. No board or tokens needed, nor computer or phone.
Beginning, I ask the person next to me, plane or party, about
themselves, then count how many questions asked before an
inquiry is returned. Regular as the yellow orb rising in the east,
almost always I reach twenty before a question is pitched about
myself. But if the business dude or young model can't unloose
themselves, I keep asking—curious to see how high the count will
go. The winner sits far above the crowd at 39—nonetheless, it's no
coincidence I advise my graduate students to spread a sweet
ganache across professional conversations by asking colleagues
and interviewers about their lives. I tell them *no one ever tires of
talking about themselves,* even if others do.

Leaf Out

It's April fifth, nine-thirty AM—fog
tongues my forearms—gifts me with
small bits of silent weather, as I run
downhill on Milledge Circle.

Every March, spring slaps me across
the cheeks, and says breathe, as I crawl
my way out of the broken egg shell
of winter.

Like my brothers-in-law, the fog speaks
in alternating voices of coldness
and warmth, and I realize it's been
months since they asked me anything
about myself.

Running downhill, through muted
air, I hear each new leaf snap
open—gasping, red oak, chalk
maple, sweetgum—as they finger-paint
the breeze with newborn greens—
mint and lime.

Today holds all the promise
of a just opened sapphire iris,
as I cross the street, reverse
course, and begin running back
uphill.

Levitation

When I was eight, a circus magician levitated
a gold-spangled, bathing beauty exactly two

hand spans above a draped green platform. Oooooh,
aaaaah. I couldn't quite grasp why hips and breasts

drew my kid-blue eyes, as if a lodestone
for the magnetic pole of all moist urges.

Trick—everyone knew, but their mouths—
open circles—said no one really cared. And isn't

that how the world now spins, belief displacing
logic and observation. Still, I wonder how

all may be levitated, not much,
just a hand span or two: a bit more food,
new clothes for the kids, a partner's
soft lips?

Turnips

Drawn from sandy black earth, skin cleansed, turnips taste like
health itself, someone doing a 10K at 70, with a

flick of bitterness for interest and effort. Agronomists
say turnips were birthed in the Hindu Kush three to six thousand

years ago—a *first vegetable*. Manipulating
evolution we have massaged them into globes, cylinders,

and discs, daubing ivory, crimson and orchid on their
palette. Purple-top white globes, Tokinashi, Hida Beni, I plant

and reap all. But my white egg turnips were unvaccinated
or lacked the multivitamin. Sickly yellowed leaves,

no bulb at all—seeds senile at age 4, apparently. A
disappointment like I was to second grade Mrs. Elliot

who said a *boy should be able to sit still.*

IRL—In Real Life

I walk up to her while she's hefting
a Bosc pear, a blushing tan orb from the produce
display at the Pig. Tammy? It's Gary Grossman,
and her arms open: a newly petaled lily enfolding
me like a plunge in Johnson's spring on a mid-July day.
A shiver climbs the beaded string of my spine, because
we've not met in real life, and I'm mildly uncertain
about the hug—tight or loose? The Pandemic etched
our friendship on virtual life (VL) rather
than RL. Yet I know her as one knows Jo March,
or Veronica Mars. Her hug was air conditioning
on a 90°F afternoon—a prayer of heart
and skin at a time when gray overpainted every color
on my palette. But honesty fits any
garment, regardless of size or material.

Torso

My fingers dance over the slab
of Bardiglio, where a bulge calls for
stripping layers of finely grained, gray
stone so her shoulders may slowly shrug
awake. The stone is a palette of gray—slate, ash,
pewter, and November, and her black veins
strike eyes with the hardness of a March fog
in Cambria. Of course the stone is imperiale.

Her future is told by running cold
water over the block—every dimple
and imperfection marked by the slow
tsunami of the frigid bath. If luck
is with me, the form remains
rather than flees.

I begin by chalking neck to thigh, then glove
and safety glass up, for the angle grinder
and diamond blade. Mask and ear plugs
seated—the vibration of a thousand rpms
shocks my forearms as marble dust sprints
to every corner. I tug down triangles and squares
of pewter stone that preserve her modesty,
until neck, shoulders, then breasts emerge from
a static silvery sea.

Decaf Espresso

Words that
should never
comingle—in
sentence or cup.

She Reads in Front of a Fake Zoom Background

So distracting: a beach on Fiji, Olympic
rainforest, or the snow-cone mountains
of the Massif Central, more beautiful
than National Geographic, and why not,
they're locked in pixel perfection, but
Gramma always told me *beauty is*
fleeting, especially when your ears
begin bobbing in and out of this
snow-capped diorama, your hair
a brown amoeba, pseudopods flailing
because no one sits totally still
while reading any poem. And I'm shuttled
back to 1966, the episode of Star
Trek where Uhuru's caught in the transporter,
protons half-here and half-other, and it takes
all my strength not to yell *Scotty, we're*
losing her, though you only have two minutes
left to read, but it just would be too, too rude.

When the Spring Winds Are Strong, Wolf Spiders Balloon

They're up on the branch tips, all eight legs en pointe—
one hundred and four chitinous arachnids, their
tutus matching leafless twigs. These spiders parse
every gust, like surfers scoping wind and swell;
desirous wind, wind strong and constant, like
the hot custard disc of June. When it blows
faithful, they hoist their buttocks, as if spiders
actually had buttocks, shooting life-lines of silk
into wind—wind, now a sculptor's hands, patting
and twirling the silk lines into a sail, or is it
a parachute; aeronauts lifting into the air
as if west was the only direction with
a street address, as if wind read their parents
faces, and agreed, only the best days are ahead.

The Price of Eggs
after Woody Allen

Family is G-d's way of keeping us humble
I like to say when asked about my relatives.

Missing Father, missing Mother, no siblings
except some halves, one of whom thinks

he's a chicken. My therapist keep suggesting
that I find him a good psychiatrist,

but my brother has no job, and we need the eggs

Crab Apples

An early snow last week,
embarrassed
the scarlet crab-apples.

Lazy fruit, now frozen,
but sweet.

Underwater

I lasted a week at the first foster home.
There I learned to only inhale, because
a completed breath brought the unknown —
days to come were milk poured into water,
cloudy and without taste, I was underwater.

The second home taught me to hold my breath —
the blue backyard plastic pool, where in June,
my bully foster brothers played octopus.
Binding arms and legs while pushing
my head under water.

Number three included parents who never
left the couch or TV — obesity, cockroaches,
and a baby boy with soiled diapers.
No AC and the thick August air
felt like breathing underwater.

Even a crazy mom beats this, so I returned
home for a year, then at 17 moved out.
Mom left LA for Tecate, Mexico, and died
eight months later, when her car vaulted
an embankment and ended up underwater.

Obituary
(Props to Victoria Chang)

Sylvia Siegel was born in Rochester NY on September 29, 1918. The daughter of Jewish immigrants, no that's not how I want to start. Sylvia Siegel married Joseph Grossman on June 1, 1951 in Manhattan, New York. They separated in October of 1953, no, that's not it either. Sylvia Siegel was killed in a car accident on Mexico Highway 2D on May 22, 1972, no, no, no. Sylvia Siegel lived fifty-four years, was mother to a loving son, and survived by her son, Gary Grossman, and her mother, Rachel Siegel. NO. Sylvia Siegel led a troubled life, perpetually trapped under the glass ceiling that held women down until the twenty-first century, and the lack of drugs for control of bipolarity, especially depression. Almost there. Sylvia Siegel...

III.

Alfalfa Hay

The fields in Farmington Georgia are checker boards;
each red square hosts a five foot cylinder of green
alfalfa hay—December fodder for hoofed four-foots.

Evenly spaced, a single bale sets sail every twenty feet
as if a sixteenth century armada of vegetal frigates
had sprung, fully formed, from the thick red clay.

The panorama is an unnatural natural, like male sage grouse
strutting feathers on a mating lek or Qin Shi's equidistant
terra-cotta warriors unearthed by Lingtong farmers.

The soothing nature of regularly spaced objects—
may my eyes continue to see
what is and what may be.

Barred Owls

The hooting begins about ten thirty,
our backyard bachelor chanting the standard
who cooks for me, who cooks for me then
ascending into a waterfall of *who ha has*
that sound like nothing so much as a
chimpanzee angered by Jim on Wild
Kingdom. A second bird flies in on
inaudible wings, and suddenly
voices braid—tight as half-inch nylon
rope, and it's clear why so many cultures
deem these alien fricative desires as
harbingers of doom—snake eyes falling
on some winter solstice night.

But my first thought is *the old boy
finally got lucky.*

History Lesson, Athens Georgia

I'm running down Antebellum Row,
Doric-columned Greek houses all painted

with the city's last stash of 1849 white-zinc
pigment. It's the straight stretch of Milledge

Avenue, named, like six other streets, after
1802 governor John, who left Heights,

Terrace, Extension, Circle, Court, and Place,
in our midst, confounding tourists trapped

for days at a single intersection. 7:37 AM,
July tenth and by mile three the soupy air

has coated my tongue with the taste of
young water oak leaves, trees that have lined

our streets for a century and now die one
by one, from the male attribute of heart

rot—fungal infidelity. My friend Bill,
town arborist, says *water oaks spend their*

first fifty years growing and their last fifty
dying but I'm unsure how this maps onto

the human storyline. At mile four, I run over
a man-hole cover dated 1916, Cobbham Iron

Works, and stoop to pick up the blue and white
surgical mask caught on the lettering—third

one this run, because history is written
by both the standing and the lost.

Pop-Up Thunderstorms

Some afternoons, sometime after two,
they swan in on crashing cymbals,
light ricocheting off polished brass,
gusts that push like the eighth grade
bully stuck too far back in line.

July in Georgia, and the heat
surfs a wave of weighted
oxygen—humidity intense
as dewy thighs, coercing me
to the sharp edge of submission.

Then, release, as if the sky
opened her refrigerator
door, and effortlessly spilled
lakes of cool liquid down upon
us—bright tears of absolution.

September should come quicker
than it does.

Folding the Sheets

My wife out of town, I manage most tasks: wipe kitchen
counters clean before bed, check basement lights,
TV shut down, and then inject myself under
a cool cotton top sheet in late June. But in
decades on this soil-iced, planet-cake,
I am outwitted each and every weekend
by my just washed, queen-size
fitted sheet. Match the corners,
match the seams, match the edges:
I fail the exam, which leads me
to the solution for all tedious
tasks. Function *must* over-
rule tradition or couture,
so I begin whirling this
sheet round and round
my forearms; a 500
thread cotton tornado,
now secretly
cavorting with
robin's egg
blue funneled
friends on the
heart-pine
shelf of
our 40's
tiled,
yellow
bathroom
closet.

Ars Poetica, Forbidden Fruit

One mile into my daily jog, New Yorker
poetry podcast in my ear, hoping for insights
and hardware to Sherpa me up poetic Olympi,
and Mary Karr is reading Terrence Hayes'
Ars Poetica with Bacon, which leads her
and host Paul Muldoon, to a number of salutary
comments on rashers, including Mary's confession
that she never ever passes up bacon, and that given
our genetic proximity to *Sus scrof*a, eating bacon
is a form of Eucharistal sacrament, although as a Jew
I'm thrown a bit by the host claim, though both Mary
and Paul (may I call you Mary and Paul) are Catholics
so they're likely correct, but this baconian discourse
reminds me of the tale of Rabbi Jacob and Priest Patrick,
lifelong friends and golfing buddies. They're sipping
a wee dram after their latest eighteen holes, because it's
always five o'clock somewhere, when Patrick
asks his friend, "tell me Jacob, have you ever broken
one of your religious precepts?" Jacob pauses a hot minute
and responds "Yes, one time I was on vacation and ate
several strips of bacon. Frankly, it wasn't anything special."
Jacob then queries Patrick—same question—Patrick replies
"I've trusted you for the thirty years of our friendship,
but for this I must insist on clerical confidentiality.
To be honest, when I was young in my vocation, and had feelings
strong as the Santa Ana Winds, I had sex with a young
widowed congregant." Jacob raises his right hand to his mouth
and whispers "It's a hell of a lot better than bacon, isn't it."
Which just goes to show, there are many experiences
that shouldn't be passed up, even if just tried once.

Remembrance

My poet friend Ted
puts names of real
people in his poems,
ensuring they live on.
And this is such a kind
sentiment, when I'd like
to forget so many—
terror apologists,
and land destroyers,
as if hate and atrocity
could be forgiven, like a
car payment or student
loan. And this construct—
that loved ones live on
in our storied memories
makes me think of
acrobats building
a body pyramid, each
memory standing on
the shoulders of the one
below. And this human
pinnacle, where would
it rest within the brain?
Would it grow inside a single
lobe, hippocampus perhaps,
or would its triangular
base splay across amygdala
and limbic lobe, atop sulci,
neurons and glial cells?
And this puzzles me, like
Nicolaas Hartsoeker's 1694
homunculus theory,
that posits a miniature
human encapsulated in
each and every sperm.
And this is the simple
physical impossibility
and miracle of it all,
the space, the cells,
the bodies, the longing.

Picking Rattlesnake Beans

Dark-roast is my first pleasure of
a July morning—then it's zoysia
wet-nuzzling my toes as I walk through
the backyard, and open the deer fence
for morning's garden harvest.

The corners of the sun's mouth turn
upwards, hands flinging a top sheet of
shortleaf pines off waking limbs—her face
chrome yellow and steaming, like ear corn
finishing in the boil.

Beans snap with lust in heat—high today 96.

Rattlesnake, a misnomer for the farmer's
faithful friend—a fail-safe bean, filling
jars stacked in any Georgia larder.

Some say they're named for coiling round
and round the vine, but not my beans—
straight and six inches long.

Parting seafoam leaves to find sheathed fruit,
minute hairs gently trace my outstretched
forearm, the tingle stretching to my spine,

it is an emerald climax.

Dead Spot

Six miles daily, half run, half walk.
Podcasts fill my ears, personal
change and poetry, then the four-way
at Highland and Catawba, where
Bluetooth lives vanish, the way an
overheated sun suddenly ducks
below world's edge on August 28th.

A dead spot, pulls up my ghosts like fog fingers
gleaning at 7:46 on a late summer morning,
then double taps the dead spot in my heart,
left by a Dad who provisioned nothing
but a name. This discomfort, variable
and diffuse, possible necrotic tissue —
maybe ventricle, maybe left atrium,
can't really tell.

Four times, endurance and the endless
sugar of magnolia blossoms helped
me bypass the township sign, Eternal Sadness;
population 72,873,628.

My daughters, neuroscientist, and
surgical vet, palpate no dead
tissue, insisting the CAT-scan
fuzz-ball is an artifact.

Still, the township sign shimmers
just above hot blacktop, maybe there,
maybe not.

Self-Portrait By Numbers

1. My stomach, furnace stoked
        with the first sips of coal
                black Mocha Java.

2. My pillows a flying butress,
        I do both Wordle
                and NYT crossword.

3. Fully awake,
        I text running buds,
                set up the daily jog.

4. Shorts,
        Asics runners,
                tank top tee

5. Scott orates history
        and upcoming travel,
                Doug, law and the farm.

6. Six miles,
        skin sags, heart races,
                85°F.

7. The small belly roll
        must go, avoiding
                medication.

8. Lunch is keto, rolled turkey
        breast dipped
                in Dijon.

9. The sorority runners were
        out today, smiles tell me
                I'm on track.

10. Sixteen ounces of iced black
        Tanzanian Peaberry fuels my
                pulse, 2:30pm.

11. Writing
    actually comes
        before the jog.

12. Post-run harvest, sweat
    drying—garden cherry tomatoes,
        & pole beans harvested.

13. Shower and dinner prep,
    today smoked trout in
        sherried cream over faro.

14. Will the belly
    roll ever wave
        goodbye?

15. Post-prandial lethargy.

16. Lying in bed,
    reading
        Tony Hillerman.

17. Wife removes book
    from my chest—
        turns out light.

18. Life
    playlist
        loops.

Picking Figs

Early today, an adult blue jay flew into the upper branches of the tree to perch, and I realized the figs were adults and ready for harvest—and then recollected how important it is to pick the first ripe figs immediately; because if I can harvest enough of these little globes just when they've turned from tannish-green to umber, I can push the avian and furred pirates out of my ocean—an essential task because their report cards are annotated *does not share well*—and they don't just consume a few figs, the small amount that would fill their grey pelted or scarlet feathered bellies, but ruin pounds of figs because some cerebral pathology has them peck each fruit, taste, *no, not this one* and move on to the next, as if the following fig will taste more heaven than earth—and so on and so on, chapter and verse—which has presented me, given that I'm a day late, with a depressing afternoon count of twenty-nine figs with small bacteria-packed cavities in the robust lower body of the fruit, the portion resembling a Rubens nude such as The Hermit and the Sleeping Angelica, painted approximately 394 years ago (rarely can one date these works precisely), but the comparison is apt—Angelica with her robust hips and thinner, relatively speaking, upper torso, absolutely resembles a fully ripe Turkish Brown fig—sides striped with pink where the flesh has overpowered the skin, venting jammy, tongue-pink pulp, and rather brazenly soliciting consumption, although that comparison is topsy-turvy.

If you own a fig tree, not that such a deeply-rooted tree can ever be owned, you likely know those *too many figs* moments, tired of jam, and tarts, and that chichi fig-prosciutto-chevre pizza, and your friends are so tired of even a whiff of the sucrosy fig smell, that they're fending you off with requests for extra zucchini, but if you can just stalemate the birds and squirrels for another nine days, the 2022 battle of the figs will be over until next summer's redemption.

Language Arts

I am considering how things classify
either as lewd or not lewd. Such a chewy
word, a mouthful, headlining tongue, lips
and jaws—a playful nip from incisors.
And colors, pink is lewd, coral is lewd,
as are rose, and raspberry. But fuchsia
and magenta, no. They bellow, in
a fake O kind of way "are you finished
yet." Just too, too, much, overdone, like
a cut of wagyu cooked well rather than
rare. Lewdness is color that pants rapidly
or oscillates without volition; the wet
whisper of wind over teeth as breath
draws in and is pushed out, mirroring
tidal flows. Subtle but hot. And odors,
musk, lewd, dried breast milk, unlewd,
six-day-old sheets, lewd, toasted bread, unlewd.

Though none of this walks my mind as my
fingers slowly flow over the unstrung pearls
of your spine.

How to Crush a Car

Grampa Abe was the scrap-metal king of Monroe,
Georgia. He began with Atlanta's rags in the 1920s,
moved on to dry goods, then got a taste of scrap

metal—rusted radiators, toasters, antique stoves.
In '47, two weeks after purchasing his first
crashed Chevy he said, "My dance card will be filled

with accidents"—and his world evolved to totaled sedans
and wagons. When wealth hit in '59 he bought a '60
Caddy, then belly laughed as he smashed it to sharp, shiny

pieces, while the Jew-excluding, old-money, country-club
barons sipped their Wild Turkey and spectated. Three years
later he threw down the gold-embossed invite, crushing it

with his heel, looked me in the eye and said,
"Some day the world will be a better place."

A Backflip of Language

Daughter number two,
toddling at twenty-three
months; strawberry-blond ringlets,
a remake of Shirley Temple.
Cornflower-blue eyes and lucid
skin—a still drying portrait
turning heads of strangers
in the vegetable aisle.

Visiting her Uncle Harald
her ears flip a summersault. His
name somehow transforms
into Uncle Horrible. Maybe
he shouldn't have done his mad-dog
growl, used for frat-boy initiations
and joke-scaring his own small sons.

Decades later he fondly
remains "Uncle Horrible,"
a nickname sticky as bubble gum
on a Macon sidewalk in July—
a spot, but not a stain.

The Wind is Lovely on August 31st

of pretty much every year, here in the
Piedmont of Georgia. Summer heat a reluctant
possum grudgingly winding its way down
Highland Avenue, turning right on South Lumpkin
and heading south out of town, while tugging
the paw of its balking younger sister,
High Humidity.

I'm still not sure how the last day of August
severs the umbilical cord of summer, and in
the process whelps autumn. Physics provides
instruction—Sol's annual lap, and an
Earth whose views are now slightly tilted.

But the striated wind—changing state to liquid,
and swirling away remnants of the month,
is my grinning dance partner. We sway
and twist, finally shedding the salt-demons of
summer.

Eleven Ways of Participating on Zoom

I.
In bed, back propped up against
two pillows wearing your alma
mater sweatshirt.

II.
With your laptop on your thighs, tilted
at forty-five degrees, so the audience
has a clear view of your nostril's contents.

III.
On your office desktop, professionally
dressed, with lots of impressive books
that you haven't read behind you.

IV.
Eating dinner so everyone will know
you eat meat and don't chew enough.

V.
After any meal with colorful food bits
protruding from between incisors
and bicuspids.

VI.
Sitting in front of a blindingly bright
window—face obscured like someone from
the anti-terrorist squad being interviewed.

VII.
With your cat walking back and forth in front
of your webcam, especially if it has
high contrast pelage such as black and white.

VIII.
With a fake background that looks like
it's trying to absorb your body
like a predatory amoeba.

IV.
With a dog by your side that keeps whining
from lack of attention and eventually dumps
on the floor, while you yell *shit, shit, shit*.

X.
Just out of the shower with a canary-yellow
towel wrapped around your damp hair,
and a partially open terry cloth robe.

XI.
Exercising on your treadmill, head
continuously bobbing up and down
like a drunken chicken.

White Oak

Headed south on Georgia 15,
on my way to Greensboro
and the lake, when the sun pours
a pillar of March light and crowns
a white oak centered in
a green-speckled field.

Stately and gray-caped; height
and belly fat say at least
300 winters. But I cannot place
the plants sprouting in that field.
I'm early for my meeting in this
mixed-use town of gentrified

geegaw stores and counter
service cafes. First stop is Reece's
Hardware, here since the '30s—
I need nails and a short-handled
hammer. The clerk's face is furrowed
like those rolled Piedmont fields.

I greet: *Hey, howya doin'*
today? His reply: *Every*
day above ground is a good day.
Our conversation moseys down
the unpaved road of country life.
I saw a beautiful old oak,

in a field west side of Eatonton
Highway 'bout five miles back—the one
with the big white mailbox. Happen
to know what that new crop is?
He replies: *this time of year*
most folks are planting alfalfa hay,

and that tree, that's the one we used
to call the hanging oak.

Sizzle

not sound but feel, when that arrow of adrenalin
flies down my arteries, vision clouds, like waking
up broken on pavement only to see
cardinal red taillights wing down the street.

Decades later I understand free-floating
anxiety sinks rather than floats, as it
slides down the birth canal of no control
a capture, by powerful other.

And my mantra becomes *this isn't really
important, you can leave at any time,*
bringing quick release, deceleration,
airplane tires hit the runway, sometimes

bouncing, sometimes not. My hands still shaking;
heart, a clanging bell, echoes off my ribs,
fear now fading, now safely tucked
for landing, underneath my seat.

Daedalus and Icarus

There is a crenulated line from Minos of Crete
to the Minotaur—product of illicit love between
Minos' wife Pasiphae and Poseidon's unsacrificed
gift—the snow white bull. Well, it occurred long ago,
different times, different customs, and Poseidon did enchant
Pasiphae, which makes me wonder if even queens had free will
then, let alone commoners. And that adjectival phrase,
snow white, which brings to mind another tale of enchantment with
multiple males, some of dubious character. But let us
return to Minos of Crete whose bride was, as they say,
steppin out, and I'm going to skip over a few minor details,
but Minos asks Daedalus to build a labyrinth, no, it
was to be The Labyrinth, unescapable by Pasiphae's son
the half-bull half-man, and anyone else. From what I hear
Daedalus barely was able to escape himself, and for this
wonder of construction, Minos imprisoned not only
Daedalus but also his boy Icarus. Well, the rest
is common knowledge, Icarus disobeys and pays,
going down in flames, as we say these days even though
it actually was going down in melted wax and loose
feathers, which may lead you to ask whether any of this
is to be believed, but fables may instruct even if inaccurate,
so when you promise a god something, make sure
you follow through.

IV.

Tante Sophie's Schnapps Glasses

These five small thimbles of 19th century
glass repose in our glazed Charleston-style,
sideboard; both shedding thin tear-trails of age,
because glass truly is a liquid, though
it takes a slightly tilted perspective
to grasp its flow.

Holding a cup to the light, I see
embedded sooty specks—remnants
of the 1890's when Cossacks sacked
Sophie's town in the Pale of Settlement—
she escaped, to Syracuse, New York.

To sack and Cossack: first cousins.

Tante Sophie's glasses emblazon
events in our embraced tribe: births,
weddings, Bar and Bat Mitzvahs.

It took me two days to realize
seven year-old Anna had taken one
to stock her American Girl Doll
kitchen.

Flipping the Switch in Georgia

Did the G-d of the South
finally begin perspiring
and give that little knob a flick,
mid-September or if lucky,
August 22nd?

Now the wind is a wave
of aloe, tonic for a stove
burned arm—a refrigerator
door held open for three cooling
minutes; humidity a dim
flicker on the retina
of summer.

And sunlight—incandescent,
like lemon icing on a just baked
wedding cake.

Autumn resurrects every
yearly cycle, but peeling off
the dried glue of summer,
my pores now greet redemption
and reconciliation, psalms
to absorb again and again.

Self-Examination

If the recession of 2008 hadn't maimed so many of us accountants, I wouldn't have started shoplifting. And though I floated towards homelessness, I clawed my way back up the economic beach, even after watching that ebb tide sweep so many bellowing colleagues out to sea. I don't mean to lack compassion, no, really, but like they say, *if ya done it, it ain't bragging.* At that point I realized my salvation lay in the collection plate of petty crime. I mean, wife and kids sayonaraed me long ago, and I've been on my own now for one hundred seventy-eight weeks.

My initiation into larceny began with basic needs stuffed down my pants—snickers bars, white bread, tins of potted meat, and pony bottles of beer, really just things to tide me over, but then a better plan skipped across my mind like the way a crumpled styrofoam cup skates over an oily canal on a windy day.

Reaching back into my old quantitative tool-bag, I began computer-scamming—targeting the idle rich, sweeping their crypto out from under their noses, while posing as a 40ish blonde widow whose nipples peered like shy buttons from a sheer black nightgown.

Twelve years later, sometimes I ask myself *do you really know the difference between want and need,* even though these economic curves are the basis of civilized capitalism? Yet neither produces the orgiastic thrill accompanying a successful theft, abdominal muscles contracting involuntarily at the start and relaxing with each exhalation as the crime struts forward.

Nonetheless, my new financial security necessitates greater self-examination, literally, more looks in the mirror, to ensure the moral portion of my face doesn't start decomposing right in front of me—like so many portraits by Francis Bacon. Which brings me to my ultimate question, can one recover from a life of property crime, and is it even necessary? I mean, doesn't society owe everyone a living, and doesn't economic inequality justify my takings? I know those are rationalizations, weak as raspberry leaf tea. Still, how much do I really need, and how much do *they* really not need, and is enough ever enough, especially given the orgasmic nature of illegitimate acquisition?

Some questions really shouldn't be asked.

Leaf Pigments

Trees speak their names: red oak and maple,
yellow poplar—obvious, no?
But red just mimes the aging shift
of emerald leaves to the dark ruby
of a '95 Diamond Hill Cabernet.

While on the topic of wine, the gingered
leaves of winged elms must be savored, like
a glass of 32 year-old Chateau d'Yquem,
but this really isn't about *la vie*
bourgeoisie modern.

Though brie and sushi bloom even on
Winn-Dixie's shelves, and Lil Nas X's Old Town
Road speaks from every diner jukebox. No—
it's about the ruddy hands of scarlet oaks
melting into wrinkled copper pennies.

And that every leaf-fall reminds
me of your passing eight years ago.

Driving Rachel to Sleep: October 1994

Sunlight plaits your hair,
then morphs into a
tangerine ball
bouncing towards me in
the rear-view mirror.

I glance up to the
reflection of a
wriggling toddler,
clasped by the indigo
arms of your new car seat.

I can't ever seem to get you down.

Seven sunset clouds
crawl by on my right,
as if they were the
last red cows returning
to the tobacco ad barn.

Your eyelids begin
to open and close —
foam atop the cobalt
waves of a small storm.

I decide to drive
further; worried that
a vagrant street lamp
will jar you awake.

Heading for home I
embrace the roads
you will travel in
the years ahead

Supply Chain Shortage

As I pour high fiber cereal into the ancestral, Melmac bowl—the shallow one permitting eyeball estimation of my half-cup ration—my brain roves the twenty-eight years, I've been eating this one cereal for breakfast, ever since unassuageable bacteria won a war with my colon and occupied a small cul-de-sac known as a diverticula. In hubris, I dub this cereal *twigs* resembling nothing as much as a pile of kindling—part derision, part acceptance, that physiologically, I now need the equivalent of a cane for my digestive tract, but like so many things in plague life, it too has fallen off the conveyor belt of supply, which has forced me to surveil local groceries hoping to unearth a box or two, perhaps underneath the Publix rainbow.

Does constancy birth tedium—or slow-rising joy?

My wife knows the truth of my imperviousness to physical elements when I'm absorbed, and last week my friend Scott said *you'll be sorry* when I stepped, thigh-high, into the 50 degree trout stream wearing pants rather than waders—but I'm never sorry when I'm standing in flowing water lined with pines, and after several hours of rainbow trout entering and exiting my net, I basked, lizard-like—on this north-south ridge overseeing October's Chattooga River, not from chills but because the sun and breeze burnished both the vireos and my inner self.

Consistency aside, tomorrow I'll buy some steel-cut oatmeal to weather this crisis.

Orphan

Raised by my single
Mom and her parents,
I've been an orphan
since they passed
in the '70s, while

Dad—a truant for every
day of father-son school,
knew me last as an
embryo:

anatomy teaches form
follows function, so
orphan really is the
right term.

Ode to My Lost Thirty Pounds

Despite my daily five miles,
I couldn't shake your clingy
arms for years, but nine months of
Ozempic turned the trick.

Now my belly hinge flops freely
even with a *suck-in*. Thank G-d
for loose running clothes,
anonymizing every droop and sag.

So many new terms to learn,
brachioplasty, bat wings,
turkey neck. Do the animals
mind these disses?

Now, my jog draws eyes—yesterday,
co-eds sheathed in fuchsia lycra.
Twin birds in mating plumage—
deserving my return of serve.

Still unaccustomed to the new
Me—shining like a newly
discovered comet circling
the neighborhood.

But it's what's inside that
counts, right? Yeah, sure.

This morning my cousin probed,
Did you get a new haircut?

Folklore

Gingko trees drop their leaves all at once,
which may be: true, partially true, or untrue,
given their cosmopolitan domestication, with
branches even here in the suburban Georgia
foothills. Google says *true*, but the gingkoes
around the corner on Catawba Drive disrobe
slowly every year, days spent with golden
kimonos only slightly open. Some say sudden
grief can turn one's hair white overnight, an
eclipse in reverse like coral bleaching, but
of course once hair climbs out of the scalp
it's dead and can't change its stripes.
Which reminds me of my sister's partner
who empties the checkbook every
month without regard to kids or food.
Like tar pits or a moth trapped in amber,
his anger forever holds himself in place.

These Days

Of blessed memory is a phrase
I'm using way too much—as too many,
of too many generations are
passing. Millennia of Jewish life
task us with this phrase, when the dark
horseman chases down one more friend,
one more relative, one more former
lover, or friend's former lover.

As a young man, this seemed trite as
velour track suits and leg warmers—
a silhouette of a rite, sans content,
like the hollow chrysalis from
a monarch butterfly I found
October fifteenth.

But now it's pandemic-life, not a
trio of days go by that I don't
grace someone with this blessing,
now a great comfort—though I'm
not exactly sure why.

Loss always is present, like the scab
that takes so long to heal, because
picking at it is a cheap ecstasy.

But *of blessed memory* is a circular
shape linking dead and alive. It is warm
milk at 2 AM—a solace that
tall or short, quiet or loud, kind or
selfish, we remain engraved on both
heart and stone.

Osmosis

It's a common party
scene, right? The cocky +1
guest who replies, from
within a rain coat of
insecurity *just joking*.

The precursor, *Yeah but
how many of these books,
have you actually
read?* Neuroses aside,
he's tapped the nail and
driven it in, as I
scan my shelves and stacks
and realize only
half of these spines have been
cracked, especially those
stacked like a high-rise with
multicolored floors.

Dust settles on shoulders
and the backs of hands as
we plan, postpone, order
that must have book while time,
an ever-present breeze, scrapes
away all soot.

I laugh and reply
*actually I'm
hoping to learn via
osmosis.*

A Gift

They home, like salmon to their
natal stream, seeking the comfort
of the only nest they've known.
Childhood neurons triggered by
beef bourguignon, baked ziti,
and bedrooms that remain undenned.

At 70 resentment still can
brush my cheeks red. Nerves quick to fire
with one more many-petaled request.
Even from one's own muscled genes.
Even when it's all years past.

But, what a gift it is when children
return home to snuggle in bed
despite their thirty-something years
and job tenure.

Soon enough we'll be cold ashes in an urn.

My Personal Relationship With the Avocado: History and Evolution

Avocado,
Alligator pear,
Avocado pear.

Avocados—birthed in
Mesoamerica, they come
from both outcrossing
and self-joy.

Avocados are relics from
an evolutionary antique
mall, no natural dispersers
left to spread their seeds.

Avocados should never
be chosen with a stem
attached—the best retain
an open wound.

Avocados were the first
veggiefruit I hated with
an intensity that only
a kid can have for food.

Avocados' texture was
the problem—sad green eggs
that refused to slide by
my tongue or taste buds.

I still hate eggs.

Avocado testing began at
twelve; perhaps puberty's
new morph flavored them
like new ice cream.

Avocados now confound
me with their ripening, like
the immaculate conception
it is faith, not science.

Avocados rest in our ash
fruit bowl, plotting their two
hour and forty seven minute
window of perfect ripeness.

Avocados—like life itself,
a moment's distraction may
flip the world upside down.

Recollections

Home on a second grade
afternoon, I sit at the small
red formica table in
Gramma's kitchen, doing
homework—inhaling thyme
and lemon from bubbling soup stock.

She said *I don't have recipes,
it's shitteryne*, a little this,
a little that,* her English still
tethered to the Pale of Settlement.

She tossed a two fingered
pinch of sour salt into chicken
stock for today's batch of shaav,
a sour grass and egg soup, straight
from her 1896 Ukrainian village.

In Rochester, no Russian
sorrel, so it's spinach, kale,
and sour salt.

Was it smell or taste that pulled
this over the transom of memory
from my hippocampal sea—no matter,
my lips are turning upwards.

*a Yiddish term meaning a little of this and a little of that

Just Fallen Leaves

Running at 70, years, not mph—my eyes sharpen
for tripping points on this frigid Thanksgiving day.
I'm forced to look down, not up—last night's
hard freeze robbed local oaks of their color
swatches—a geometric collage atop a frosted
concrete canvas: magenta and crimson, paling
to tepid beige. Now, as ice crystals yield to a late
autumn sun, my steps also fade to a slow lope—
fear not of flying but, falling, which I suppose is
a form of slow flight. Looking down, I imagine
Autumn's hands slowly caressing these leaves
from the tree's thighs, and remember how we
made love when you returned last Tuesday.

Objects in Mirror Are Closer Than They Appear

My casual remark that unknowingly wounds the friend,
who parks her heart on the den mantle next to her son's urn.

My first love who left for financial solvency.

My oldest son who stormed off weekly; the red tide
of anger has aged off his face.

My mid-afternoon Macintosh apple core thrown
completely over the trash basket.

My now forgotten promise that I would pick up pizza
on my way home from the bookstore.

My neighbor who tried to move his property line six
inches over mine.

My youngest daughter who could amuse herself
at eleven months.

It's all closer than you think.

Cohabitation

Moths, unnerving as a loose power line flailing
the jello air with high voltage, as it is their
randomness that frightens, erratically bouncing up
to down, right to left, northeast to southwest—I miss swat
after swat as if these small, powdery planes had ESP
or echolocation. I've lived years with these carpet
and clothing moths, Tricophaga, Tinea, and Tineola.
Gnawers of suits and carpets, shearing stitches like
the anti-seamstress. Not willing to bomb the
house we coexist, Latvia and Russia, as I rocket
off the couch while watching Jimmy Kimmel—trying
to forecast the spins and barrel rolls of this latest
lepidopteran dogfighter—my weapon, hand or blue
plastic swatter. Sometimes the rush of success—then I lick
talc-dusted fingers, erasing the chalky corpse from
the ecru living room wall. Next morning, I open
my tee shirt drawer, only to unveil two tiny holes
in my AthFest 2015 shirt, the one perfectly
aged, sweet as a baby's bum, and I reckon that
moth-human interactions are eternal as sunrise
in the east, an unwinnable war against survivors
of the Age of Insects, unless I'm willing to invoke
the nuclear option—but the holes are small
and few will notice.

Missing

For three weeks, house & chores—mine alone, Barb ensconced
at the little toe of San Francisco Bay, now helping her
final sister up the crooked stairway—chemo and radiation.

I pull a week's worth of musty flannel sheets off our
marital bed, to find a tracing of Barb's outstretched
arms and legs; four decades, a faint K remains.

Shopping and vacuuming both, now too tired to cook,
I smile at the purchased roll of tunamaki, like me,
the rice is geriatric—a "sell by" bargain.

Watering and harvesting our garden's winter bounty:
lettuce, kale, scallions, carrots, bok choi, and mizuna.
Wash, rinse, refrigerate.

My eyes tire, vision drifts, as I wonder, which of us
will end up in the solitaire setting?

The Funeral

At the gym, he waved me over, and when I said
No, I'm not going he cocked his liver-spotted head
to the left, mouth, now opening and closing
like a fish wanting back in the pond—as if my
declaration forced him to unstitch the previous
eleven seconds, his pupils dilating, unfocused,
but now fixing on some obligation lurking ten
feet behind my head.

I'm done with funerals.

What duty do I have to someone on the job
for twenty-five years, who wrote only blank pages
of conversation? Colleague? Co-worker? Associate?
Someone who rebuffed all intimacy, as if
children, spouses and beer didn't exist.

Glancing at a now vacant weight-bench, I tried to reel
him back in—*we weren't any kind of friends you know,
just two people who worked on the same floor for years.*

Final Frost

At seventy, it's all odds, even planting veggies.
Sage of the Georgia almanac says *Last frost,*

fifteenth of April—plant prior, and clay-red hands spin
the roulette wheel—odds slightly less than fifty-fifty

(green zero and double zero). Will sprouts have
a funeral in crystalline shrouds, or early births of

tomatoes, peppers, and beans. Seeds are a hold-em
promise from Gaia—because life is both poker

and blackjack—draw two and hit me again—they're
just plants though.

And my own final frost?

Flight 348, Atlanta to Sacramento

Glancing over at the Gen Zer sporting crimson stilettos,
kitty corner from me in seat 23C, I notice the brim
of her ball cap is pinned with crossed rifles. My regard soars
given she's a military sharpshooter, but when my glasses
post, the rifles morph into fairy wings and outstretched legs
along with other fairy miscellanea, done in steel-colored
embroidery, which makes me wonder whether I really
should have confessed to the lady next to me, in 24E,
that I closed the overhead bin indicating it was full;
even though with four hard thrusts, she was able
to force in one more paramecium-like bag
and a purple nylon rain coat, all the while issuing
wren-like *tsks* about *"those selfish folks who close
overhead bins when they're not full."* But my fear
of damaged items is legit—I have four 80-year-old
fountain pens sequestered in my semi-soft carry-on.
Pens glowing with the wisdom of lined hands
that turned antique celluloid, and the certainty
of *Art Deco* and Parker permanent blue-black ink.
Scanning forward, I'm abruptly flown back to 1982,
because this chaste Airbus 320 from Toulouse
has a smoking/no-smoking symbol above every seat,
which makes me wonder, if any country is so uncaring
it still allows smoking on commercial jets? Then the corners
of my mouth tug themselves upwards, preventing me
from saying aloud *"how very French this is"*,
while my pancreas exudes a small hit of insulin-based tranquility,
and I realize that sometimes, contentedness is as simple
as suddenly noticing the seven-month-old baby
in the row behind me, who slept through the entire flight—
her lips, swallow's wings set in a simple dreamy smile.

Acknowledgements

These poems were previously or will soon be published in these literary reviews

Chewers by Masticodores—Decaf Expresso, Softness, Final Frost, Leaf Pigments,

Chiron Review—Guy in a Thin Blue Parka Doing Tai Chi in the Last Available Parking Spot in the Restaurant Lot

Defenestration—Eleven Ways of Participating on Zoom.

Delta Poetry Review—Alfalfa Hay

Eunoia Review—Torso

Full House– The Mockingbird and the Worm

Jackdaw Review—Permanence

Last Stanza Poetry Journal—Driving Rachel to Sleep 1994, Pulling Carrots as Picking Carrots, Just Fallen Leaves, Athens, GA

Libre—Sizzle

Lothlorien Poetry Journal—Orphan, The Price of Eggs

MacQueen's Quinterly—A Backflip of Language, Barred Owls, Covering the Beds, How to Crush a Car, One Degree of Separation, Picking Figs, Rising at 5:47am, Tante Sophie's Schnapps Glasses, White Oak, Cohabitation, She Reads in Front of a Fake Zoom Background, and Folklore

Masticodores Chewers—Decaf Espresso, Final Frost, Leaf Pigments, Softness

Medusa's Kitchen—Ars Poetica, Cloacal Kiss, Self-Examination, Underwater

Midwest Poetry Review—Crab Apples

One Sentence Poems—Impulse Control

Panoplyzine—Frog Shrouded

Poetry Breakfast—Recollections

Poetry Superhighway—Flight 348, Atlanta to Sacramento

Rat's Ass Review—Adolescence

Red Wolf Editions Wondrous Leaflets—Toxicity, Objects in Mirror Are Closer Than They Appear, Self-Portrait by Numbers

Salvation South—Bare Bones, Leaf Out, The Wind is Lovely on August 31st, History Lesson, Athens, GA

Streetlight—Bloodroot in March, Flipping the Switch, When Spring Winds Are Strong Wolf Spiders Balloon

Tiny Seed Literary Journal — My Personal Relationship With the Avocado: History and Evolution

The Beatnik Cowboy — The Funeral, Will You Buy My Book

The Prose Poem — Truth Matters, Polar Vortex, The Anger of a Slapped Sky, Artifact

Verse Virtual — Bruised Old Apples (under the title Trauma), Chicken Truck, Folklore, Dead Spot, Missing, Osmosis, Picking Rattlesnakes, Sprouting Onions, The Gift, These Days, Levitation, Pop-Up Thundershowers.

Cultural Daily — MRI

First Literary Review-East — Obituary

Box of Matches Literary Journal — Magic

Biography

Gary Grossman is Professor Emeritus of Animal Ecology at University of Georgia, and an author of 150+ scientific articles that have been cited over 9800 times. Gary has poems, short fiction and essays in over 70 literary reviews including: *Streetlight, Verse-Virtual, Sheila-Na-Gig, MacQueen's Quinterly, Salvation South, Meat for Tea: the Valley Review Verse-Virtual, Rust and Moth*, and Delta Poetry Review. His poetry and short fiction have been nominated for a Pushcart and Best of the Net (2) with one nomination pending. For 10 years he wrote the "Ask Dr. Trout" column for American Angler Magazine. Gary's poetry books *Lyrical Years* (Kelsay), *and What I Meant to Say Was...* (Impspired Press), are available from Amazon. His 2023 graphic memoir *My Life in Fish—One Scientist's Journey...* (Impspired) and his gourmet venison cookbook *A Bone to Pick* also may be purchased from Amazon.

Website: www.garygrossman.net

Poet Gary Grossman has done it again! He's written another fabulous collection of poems that left me wanting more. "Kale cultivars embrace frost, and their sage-green to rosy bodies makes them as luscious as freshly licked nipples on an arching chest," the poet proclaims in "Covering the Beds." Grossman's unique style and POV are impressive, and make this book a must read.
—Alexis Rhone Fancher, author of *Brazen, Triggere*d, and *The Dead Kid Poems*

Gary Grossman's poems combine a scientist's cool detachment with a poet's intense yearning to create a voice uniquely his own. He looks back at a traumatic childhood with clarity and compassion, and at the complexities of everyday experience with humor and wisdom. Broadly speaking, the poems focus on the wonder of life and the inevitability of death in the human and the natural worlds. More specifically, they address the poet's awareness of his own aging and mortality, which is always closer than it appears.
—Eric Nelson

In *Objects in Mirror May Be Closer Than They Appear*, poet Gary Grossman uses mirror and microscope to observe the closer-than-you-think past. With equal care, he analyses outer layers of pretense, disguise, and skin. Combining the personal and the scientific, he sees beyond the moment. "Even in poetry," Grossman explains, "genius begins as atoms no one else has cleaved." Filled with birds, gardening, and mating, Objects in Mirror addresses—in prose poems and free verse—the humorous and the heady. The poet moves easily from decaf espresso, Zoom poetry readings, and old Woody Allen jokes to his mother's bipolar disorder, bully foster brothers, and a collapsing spinal cord. As Grossman states, "My wife says I'm less bruised than most old apples." He suggests aging is "a matter of survival," a claim made with rejoicing and resignation. Yet these poems, both tart and sweet, are ripe and ready for the picking. Enjoy.
—Marjorie Maddox, author of *Seeing Things*

There is a lot to admire in Gary Grossman's work in general, and in *Objects in Mirror May Be Closer Than They Appear* in particular. He deals with life and the world with sensitivity and insight. He sees through artifice and lies brilliantly, and he gives us moments of great beauty. But many poets can do this. What distinguishes Grossman's work is that he has the soul of a poet, but the education and training of a scientist. He understands what great nature poets all understand, that the beauty and magic of nature is contained in the science that describes it. He unlocks the magic of nature for us. Through his work, we understand the intricacies of the natural world, but with his poet soul, he shows us the natural world with grace.

—John Brantingham, former Poet Laureate of Sequoia and Kings Canyon National Parks